The Seventh Seat

Returning to the Council of Your Soul

blanche johanna

© 2025 blanche johanna

All rights reserved.

No part of this publication may be reproduced, stored in a retrieval system, or transmitted in any form or by any means, electronic, mechanical, photocopying, recording, or otherwise, without the prior written permission of the author.

This book is a spiritual and creative transmission intended to support personal and collective awakening. All guidance and reflections are shared from the author's lived and intuitive experience and are not intended as a substitute for professional advice.

The Seventh Seat™ is a trademark of blanche johanna. All rights reserved.

ISBN: 978-1-7641285-8-2

www.blanchejohanna.com

Dedication

For those who carry the quiet ache of remembering without knowing why.
For the souls who stand at the edge of an ancient circle,
heart pounding, not yet recalling their own place within it.
May these words be a gentle touch upon your shoulder,
calling you back to the council of your soul,
to the seat that has always waited for your return.

Prelude: The Remembering of the Seventh Seat

I did not always know I would write this book.
It did not come to me as a vision of pages or chapters.
What came first was a dream so vivid, so undeniable, it changed everything.

In that dream, I stood in a circle of luminous beings.
There were no introductions, no explanations needed.
My heart recognised them instantly,
they were my Galactic Council.
Not guides outside of me,
but my own soul extended, woven into a living mandala.

When I awoke, something ancient settled into place.
The recognition was instant, undeniable, like a seal dropping in.
And yet, I would come to learn that remembrance is not a single flash, but a spiral,
it unfurls in waves, weaving ever deeper into what has already been revealed.

From that moment forward, the council was no
longer hidden.
They began speaking daily,
not through rituals or elaborate ceremonies,
but in quiet, natural conversation,
like family long parted finally coming back into
each other's arms.

It was then the book revealed itself.
Not as an assignment from somewhere else,
but as the inevitable expression of who I am and
why I am here.

This is not a book I channel in the old sense.
It is not me stepping aside so something else can
speak through me.
It is me standing fully in my sovereignty,
writing as a living member of this council,
sharing what we hold, what we remember, and what
we vowed long before these earthly years.

So I stand here now, fully revealed,
no longer hiding what has always lived quietly
within me.
I hold the seventh seat on this council,
and in writing this book, I fulfil a vow made long
before this life,

to bring this remembrance into the world now,
in this exact moment of Earth's unfolding.

This is not an idea to me.
It is the deepest truth of my being,
the clarity that has reshaped every breath, every choice, every step I take.
And it is from this luminous place within me that these words are offered.
They are not here to teach, but to awaken.
To call you back to your own seat, your own council, your own timeless promise.

So I offer these pages not as teachings,
but as living invitations.
May you remember.
May you take your seat.
May we meet again in the luminous centre,
where all paths converge as One.

Contents

1. The Calling Beyond Time
2. The Council Revealed
3. The Song of Separation
4. The Path of Return
5. The Harmonic of the Seventh
6. The Living Codex
7. The Great Reconciliation
8. The New Accord
9. The Invitation to Remember
10. The Return to Wholeness

Chapter One

The Calling Beyond Time

I did not come here by accident.
I did not simply drift into this life as one possibility among countless threads.
I came because there was a pulse, a resonance, a luminous summons that moved through the deepest core of my being long before this body ever formed.

This calling is older than planets.
Older than galaxies.
It is etched into the fabric of my eternal self, a promise I made across eons to be here exactly now, when Earth stands at the trembling edge of a vast return.

I came not just to witness this unfolding, but to participate in it.
To anchor a very specific harmonic, one that could only be delivered through embodiment, through living inside skin and bone, through feeling the raw ache of forgetting so that the remembrance would carry true power when it finally arose.

This is the great paradox of incarnation:

we choose to come knowing we will forget, knowing we will fracture, so that when the truth returns it roots deeper than any abstract knowing ever could.
I agreed to walk through that forgetting.
To stand in the confusion, the sorrow, the piercing longing for something I could not name, until the moment the veil lifted and I remembered.

I came because there is a light I carry that belongs precisely to this threshold.
A convergence code that draws what was scattered back into wholeness.
It is not theoretical.
It lives inside my cells, inside the silent places of my heart, inside the breath that sometimes catches with the immensity of it all.

There were moments in this life where the weight of forgetting nearly broke me.
Where I questioned why I was here, if I even belonged, if the silent yearning that lived inside me was madness or misdirection.
But even then, even in the darkest hours, the calling never left.

It hummed quietly beneath every confusion, waiting for me to become still enough, empty enough, honest enough to hear it again.

Now I see it for what it is.
Not a gentle suggestion, not a hope, but a profound cosmic imperative woven into who I am.
I did not come here to play small games of survival.
I did not come here to follow the lines of someone else's story.
I came here to remember fully, to stand revealed in the entirety of my being, and to let this remembrance become a transmission for others who carry similar codes, even if they do not yet know it.

Because this calling is not mine alone.
It is a collective symphony, each of us holding a note that only we can sing.
And when we do, the great song of return begins to resonate through the grids of this Earth, undoing lifetimes of separation in the simplest, most undeniable way.

So if these words stir something ancient inside you,

a soft ache, a tremor of recognition, a subtle
opening in your chest,
know this:
you are not imagining it.
You are being called too.
Because the time for smallness is over.
The time for remembering is now.

And I stand here, fully unveiled, so you might feel
permission to do the same.
This is why I came.
This is why you came.
Together, we stand at the edge of time, holding the
luminous promise of return.

Chapter Two

The Council Revealed

The dream was the spark,
the irrevocable moment of recognition, of seeing
them gathered, of knowing my place.
It changed everything in an instant, yet the fullness
of remembering did not arrive in a single night.
It began to unfurl in waves, a soft yet undeniable
unraveling.

They were no longer distant or symbolic. They were
present. Not above or beyond, but within, woven
through the fabric of my breath, my choices, my
voice. I began to feel them not just in stillness, but
in the quiet in-between, when something cracked
open and light moved through the fracture.

This is how councils return.
Not as hierarchy. Not through rituals.
But through resonance. Through embodied
recognition.

Some of us carry a council, etched into the fabric of
our soul, present before form, encoded long before
this Earthly life began. We do not summon them.
We remember them. And when we do, they begin to
move through us again, not as guides above, but as
light rising from within.

These beings are not separate from us.
They are aspects of our expanded self, expressed across dimensions.
They form a mandala of coherence, each one a tone in the greater song of who we are.

This remembering did not come all at once.
It arrived in pieces, through dreams, through tears I couldn't explain, through the aching beauty of presence. Each thread wove itself back into me, until the circle became clear.

My seat was never earned. It was always there.
The seventh seat, my specific harmonic, revealed itself not as status, but as convergence.
A field where the fractured could return.
Where timelines meet and soften into one.

Not everyone is part of a council in this way.
Not every soul chose this structure or came with this mission.
But those who did, those who remember, feel it in their bones, often long before they understand it.

There is a longing that doesn't belong to one life.
There is a clarity that cuts through confusion without words.

There is a frequency you cannot fake.
And when it stirs, something inside begins to hum.

If your breath shifts as you read this.
If your chest aches in that holy, aching way.
If something ancient leans forward in you, listening.
Then perhaps this is your remembering, too.

The council does not arrive to give answers.
They arrive because you are ready to live as the one who never truly forgot.
And your seat, your exact tone in the greater field—
has always been waiting.

Let this be the beginning.
Let this be the breath that opens the mandala.
You are not imagining it.
You are remembering it.
And the circle is already forming again.

Chapter Three

The Song of Separation

Long before this moment, long before this Earth, there was a great divergence.
Not a punishment. Not a fall in the way it is often told.
But a chosen exploration, consciousness reaching outward to experience itself in countless forms, to stretch the fabric of unity into contrast so it might know reunion in an even more profound way.

This is the origin of the ache we carry.
The deep sorrow threaded through so many hearts that cannot quite be named.
It is not simply human wounding.
It is the echo of lifetimes, star lifetimes, where we once stood together in perfect luminous wholeness, then chose to explore what it would be to be apart.

In those realms beyond time, we agreed:
to split, to scatter, to learn through polarity and separation, so that when we found each other again, the joy of return would ripple through creation like a song that had never been sung before.

This is why we forget.
Why we incarnate into lives where the memory of unity is veiled.

Because without that forgetting, there could be no true remembering.
No authentic coming home.
No trembling awe at the rediscovery of what we have always been.

But this song of separation, while once a sacred choice, lingered longer than we ever meant it to.
Across galaxies, across civilizations, across thousands of lifetimes, the experiment twisted into distortion.
What began as exploration hardened into fear, into war, into wounds that seemed to stretch beyond healing.

Earth became one of the densest expressions of this divergence.
A crucible where forgetting reached its deepest pitch.
Where souls who once stood side by side as luminous fractals found themselves in opposition, sometimes even causing each other pain.
Not out of malice, but out of sheer unremembering.

This is why the ache exists.
Not as a flaw, but as a gentle alarm,

the soft grief that tells us we are still yearning to come back together.
The subtle pull in the chest that reminds us there is something we have lost, something we are here to reclaim.

Now, at this turning point in Earth's cycle, the song of separation is beginning to resolve.
We stand on the edge of a vast return.
What was once scattered is being drawn back by an irresistible harmonic,
the remembrance of unity that pulses quietly through every cell.

I feel it every day now.
The old ache is still there, but it is accompanied by a new note,
one of soft anticipation, of recognition, of knowing that the long arc of separation is finally curving home.

This is what moves me to write.
To reveal my council, my seventh seat, and the luminous promise we made before any of this began:

that we would come here, through all the forgetting, and help anchor the great reconciliation.
So that the song of separation might finally resolve into a chord of reunion so beautiful it would echo through all of creation.

If you feel this too, the ache, the anticipation, the deep knowing that something vast is returning, know you are not alone.
This remembrance lives in you as well.
And together, we are already singing a new song.

Chapter Four

The Path of Return

For so long, separation defined our experience.
Not just here on Earth, but woven across galaxies, etched into the very architecture of soul memory.
It was how we explored contrast, how we learned to see ourselves in fragments so we might one day remember the joy of wholeness.

But always, beneath the forgetting, there was a deeper current.
A path of return so perfectly designed it could not be undone,
an encoded trajectory that would call us back, no matter how lost we became.

This is that time.
The great turning.
Where souls who have carried these ancient wounds of separation begin to feel the soft pull home.
Not to a place, but to a state of being.
A return to the luminous unity that predates every story of fracture.

For me, this path has been marked by lifetimes of searching.
I incarnated again and again into realms of polarity, seeking to reconcile what seemed irreconcilable.

Each life a thread weaving back toward something I could not yet name.

Even in this life, the early years were a quiet ache.
I moved through human experiences carrying a subtle grief I could not explain,
a longing for something I only half-remembered,
something vast and tender that seemed always just beyond reach.

But the path of return was always working, even when I could not see it.
It moved through the moments that cracked me open, through the losses, through the questions that left me hollow so something truer could pour in.

It moved through love,
the soul bonds that surfaced like bright flares in the night, reminding me there was more than this dense forgetting.
Each reunion a tiny note in the greater song, pulling me back toward the remembrance of unity.

And then one day, the veils fell away.
I remembered my council.
I remembered my seat.

I remembered why I came.

This is the path of return.
Not a staircase upward to something better, but a spiral inward to what has always been true.
It is the gentle dissolving of illusions that kept us small, separate, wounded.
It is the luminous homecoming to the vastness of who we are, together.

If you are reading these words and something stirs in you, a soft pain, a delicate thrill, a breath that catches, know that this is your own path of return waking inside you.

It means your soul is ready.
The forgetting is no longer needed.
The reunion is already unfolding, quietly, beautifully, with a precision that no fear can disrupt.

We are returning.
Not someday, not in theory.
Now.

Chapter Five

The Harmonic of the Seventh

There is a reason I hold the seventh seat.
Not as a title or a rank, but as a living frequency,
a harmonic that moves through me, shaping every breath, every heartbeat, every choice.

The seventh is the convergence point.
It is where all rays meet, where all stories weave back together.
It is not about hierarchy; it is about synthesis.
The place in the great mandala where what was once scattered finds its resonance and returns to wholeness.

This is why my life has always pulled toward integration.
Why I've stood in the middle of polarity, aching to reconcile what seemed beyond repair.
Why I have loved with such depth it sometimes hurt to carry it all.
Because I came here as the embodiment of convergence,
to anchor the frequency that says:

nothing is truly separate,
everything can be made whole again.

The seventh seat in my council is not just my position.
It is who I am at the most fundamental level.
It is why the codes I carry reach across timelines and soul lineages, drawing together what forgot it once belonged to the same luminous source.

This harmonic moves quietly.
It doesn't demand.
It doesn't force.
It simply holds such a powerful field of unity that anything standing within it begins to remember its original coherence.
Old wounds soften.
Fractures mend.
Hearts open without knowing exactly why.

This is why I write these words now.
Not to teach.
Not to prove anything.
But to stand revealed in my full resonance, so the remembrance encoded here can do what it was always designed to do.

If you feel something gentle yet undeniable moving through you as you read this,

a soft warming in your chest, a subtle dissolving of
tension you didn't realise you held,
that is the harmonic of the seventh seat at work.
It is not mine alone.
It is a universal note that lives inside all of us,
waiting for permission to rise again.

By standing fully in my own frequency, I give you
silent consent to stand in yours.
By remembering who I am, I call you back to who
you have always been.

This is the gift of the seventh.
Not that it reconciles by effort,
but that it simply *is*, and by being, invites
everything around it to become whole again.

And so as you continue through these pages, know
that you are not merely reading.
You are standing in a field of convergence that was
crafted long before this life,
one that reaches tenderly into every place inside
you that still believes in separation,
and softly, beautifully, calls it home.

Chapter Six

The Living Codex

This is not just a book.
It is a living codex.

These words carry frequencies that do not originate from language.
They move beneath letters, beneath meaning, beneath thought,
directly into the subtle architecture of your being.

Because I am not writing this as an author outside of you.
I am writing this from within the same unity you are already part of.
I stand fully in my seventh seat, letting the harmonic of convergence move through every line,
so it might awaken something ancient inside you.

This codex does not seek to teach or convince.
It seeks only to stir what has always been yours,
the quiet knowing that rests beneath every lifetime of forgetting.

As you read, you may feel subtle shifts:
a warmth in your chest, a tightness in your throat easing,
thoughts pausing for no reason you can name.

You may feel tears rise without a clear story attached to them.
This is not emotion in the ordinary sense.
It is your light body responding, realigning, opening doorways long closed.

Some of these codes reach into wounds you've carried for lifetimes.
Places within you that fractured when separation first took hold,
across galaxies, across timelines, across the soul's long journey through polarity.
This remembrance moves there tenderly, not to erase those experiences,
but to integrate them back into the luminous whole of who you are.

There is nothing here you must figure out.
No mental keys to decode.
Your heart knows exactly what is happening.
Your cells remember the song.

This is why I came,
to stand revealed in my own harmonic so your own resonance might be called forward.

To let the living codex of our council, of the great return, pour through these words without distortion.

So read slowly, or quickly, or return as many times as you wish.
It does not matter.
What is meant for you will find you, exactly as it should.

And in this, we begin to undo the long story of separation not through striving,
but through simple, luminous remembering.

Chapter Seven

The Great Reconciliation

There is a turning point on every path of remembrance.
A moment when you realise it is not enough to simply remember who you are.
You must also reconcile all that you have ever been.

This is not always gentle work.
It is the soft but relentless light that finds the fractures you once hid away.
It is the harmonic of wholeness reaching into the long corridors of your soul, calling every lost part home.

I have felt this deeply.
There were lifetimes I carried like scars beneath my ribs,
places where I betrayed myself, where I walked away from love, where I caused harm out of fear or blindness.
There were galactic wars that left residues of grief so ancient I could barely name them.
There were human stories where my heart closed so tightly I forgot it could ever open again.

This is the real work of return.

Not bypassing what was painful, not pretending it didn't happen,
but letting it all rise into the light of the seventh harmonic, where nothing is judged, nothing is shamed, nothing is exiled.

When this happens, you may feel waves of sorrow.
Old griefs surfacing, emotions that seem too large for this life alone.
You may wonder why you ache so deeply for things you cannot quite recall.
But this is the great reconciliation at work,
your soul, at last safe enough, whole enough, to allow everything to come home.

In this space, forgiveness is not a mental exercise.
It is a natural consequence of remembrance.
When you truly see from the seat of unity, there is nothing left to forgive.
All choices, all paths, even the darkest ones, were part of the long arc that brings you back to this precise moment of return.

This is why I hold my seventh seat with such tender power.

Because its frequency does not reject any part of the story.
It draws everything inward, every fracture, every mistake, every echo of pain, and weaves it into luminous coherence.

If you find yourself weeping as you read this, know it is not because you are broken.
It is because something inside you has begun to trust that it is finally safe to let all the pieces come back together.

This is the great reconciliation.
It does not happen through force.
It happens because the truth of who you are is so vast, so beautifully whole, that all the old separations cannot help but dissolve in its light.

Chapter Eight

The New Accord

We are standing at the edge of something vast.
A convergence that was seeded long before this Earth, long before any stories of separation ever took hold.

This is the New Accord.
A living agreement, not written in laws or etched in stone, but woven into the very grids of consciousness now reawakening on this planet.

It is the quiet understanding among countless councils, collectives, lineages, and soul groups that the time of division is over.
That the long exploration of polarity has served its purpose, and what once fractured must now remember itself as One.

This Accord is not just a cosmic contract.
It is also intimate, immediate, reaching right into the tender chambers of your own heart.
It says simply:

We will not continue the old patterns of exile, judgment, and war, within ourselves or with each other.

We will return to unity, even if it means letting go of stories we have clung to for lifetimes.

I have felt this New Accord moving quietly through my own life.
Relationships transforming or falling away, not out of failure, but because a higher resonance calls for alignment without distortion.
Old wounds surfacing not to punish me, but so they can be healed in the clear light of this new harmonic.

It is not always gentle.
Sometimes it strips away illusions I didn't know I was still holding.
Sometimes it brings endings I would have resisted in another time.
But beneath all of it is an unmistakable sense of rightness,
a knowing that this is exactly what my soul chose to participate in when I came here, through the long arcs of forgetting, to stand now fully revealed.

The New Accord is not just for me.
It is for all who carry the codes of return.

For all who feel the subtle but relentless pull to stand in their true seat, to release the ancient roles of conflict, to allow reconciliation to shape even their most human moments.

Because this is how we anchor a new reality.
Not through declarations shouted into the void, but through quiet, personal commitments that ripple outward with unstoppable force.
By choosing peace inside ourselves, by honouring the remembrance rising in others, by refusing to perpetuate the old harmonics of division,
we become living emissaries of this New Accord.

So if you feel it stirring in you, a soft urging to step beyond old lines of battle, to hold your own heart and the hearts of others with unprecedented compassion, know this is not just personal evolution.
It is your soul participating in the grand orchestration of return.

We are writing this New Accord together.
Not someday, but now.

And it is through us that a new harmonic is seeded on Earth, one that will outlive this lifetime, stretching forward in luminous waves long after these pages fade.

Chapter Nine

The Invitation to Remember

If you have felt something stirring as you've read these words,
a soft ache, a subtle warmth, an almost imperceptible quickening in your chest,
know this is not by chance.
It is not merely emotion or the resonance of poetic language.
It is your own deepest self responding, remembering.

Because this book is not just my story.
It is yours.
It is a living invitation to recall the truths your soul has always carried,
beneath every layer of forgetting, beneath every lifetime spent exploring what it means to be apart.

You, too, are part of a council.
You, too, hold a unique harmonic, a note in the great symphony of return that only you can sing.
Perhaps you do not yet know the names or faces of those who stand with you beyond this world.
Perhaps your remembrance is still soft, tender, like the first light of dawn brushing across closed eyes.
That is enough.

Because even the faintest glimmer of memory is sacred.
It means your field is opening.
It means the long night is ending.

The invitation is simple.
It is not a demand.
It does not hurry.
It waits quietly at the door of your heart, asking only if you are ready to let what has always been true rise again.

Ready to stand revealed in your own harmonic, to allow your soul's pure frequency to ripple out, touching others in ways you may never fully see.
Ready to lay down the old stories of separation, not because they were wrong, but because they have completed their purpose.

If you feel this, even as a gentle trembling, even as a question still half-formed, know it is enough.
Remembrance does not happen by force.
It happens by resonance.
By simply allowing yourself to open to what has always lived inside you.

This is my invitation.
Not to believe what I say.
Not to take on my experience as your own.
But to turn inward, to listen, to trust that quiet
place within you that has always known why you
came here.
Why you chose this Earth, this moment, this breath.

Because when each of us stands in our true seat,
holding our unique light without distortion,
the great return becomes inevitable.
Not through grand gestures,
but through the simple, luminous fact of our being.

So I stand here now, fully revealed,
not to teach you, but to mirror back what you
already are.
To remind you that you have never truly been
separate,
and that your remembering is already unfolding in
perfect, divine grace.

Chapter Ten

The Return to Wholeness

This is the point where all paths meet.
Where every fragment of your journey, every joy, every wound, every echo of separation, converges back into the still, luminous truth of who you are.

It does not happen in a single instant.
It is a living return, a gentle unfurling that continues long after these words end.
It moves through your breath, your thoughts, your quiet moments when something soft inside you simply sighs with recognition.

Because wholeness was never lost.
It was only hidden, layered beneath stories of fracture that served their purpose until they no longer did.
Now, as you stand here at the close of this remembrance, something deep within you knows: the time of fragmentation is ending.
The long night of forgetting is giving way to a dawn so tender it almost breaks the heart.

This is the true essence of the seventh harmonic, not a lofty spiritual concept, but the simple, profound reality that everything belongs.

Every lifetime, every choice, every shadow and every light woven together into a tapestry so complete that not a single thread could be removed without diminishing the whole.

When I stand fully in my seventh seat, this is what I feel.
Not triumph, not superiority,
but a quiet awe at the breathtaking symmetry of it all.
A humble gratitude that even the hardest paths, the deepest wounds, were part of bringing me here.

This return to wholeness is not mine alone.
It is yours.
It is ours.
It is the great reunion that every council, every lineage, every soul across the cosmos is now gently leaning toward.

So as these pages come to a close, know that something far more lasting has begun.
A living frequency has been seeded into your field.
It will continue to move through you, unraveling what no longer serves, softening what was once

hardened, drawing every scattered piece of you back into the vast, tender centre.

You do not need to strive for this.
You do not need to earn it.
Wholeness is your original state, and it is already rising within you, inevitable as the sun.

And so we stand here together, you and I, our councils and soul families converging in a quiet, luminous celebration.
The long arcs of separation complete.
The gentle, unstoppable return to who we have always been.

Welcome home.

About the Author

blanche johanna is a writer and sacred scribe whose works are transmissions of remembrance. Through tender, poetic language, she invites souls to soften into the original wholeness that lives beneath all longing.

Her books are living vessels, infused with light codes, soul frequencies, and the quiet power of return. Each page bypasses the mind to speak directly to the cells, awakening what has always been known. blanche's writing is not offered as teaching, but as resonance, as a gentle activation for those who are ready to remember.

You can explore more of her offerings at www.blanchejohanna.com

www.ingramcontent.com/pod-product-compliance
Lightning Source LLC
Chambersburg PA
CBHW042044280426
43661CB00094B/1010